CONTENTS

INTRODUCTION

Environmental education has an important contribution to make to the work of schools in promoting the spiritual, moral, and cultural development of pupils and of society, and preparing pupils for the 'opportunities, responsibilities and experiences of adult life', as required by Section One of the Education Reform Act (1988).

This booklet is designed to support schools in planning and teaching environmental matters through National Curriculum subjects and religious education for pupils aged from five to 16*. However, environmental matters also have an important contribution to make in both pre-school and post-16 education.

The booklet is intended for headteachers and governors, senior managers, subject leaders and teachers.

SCAA hopes that the ideas and examples of effective practice set out in these pages will support the work of schools both in meeting their statutory obligations and, where they so choose, in moving beyond them.

AIMS

Environmental education aims to:
- provide all pupils with opportunities to acquire the knowledge, understanding and skills required to engage effectively with environmental issues, including those of sustainable development;
- encourage pupils to examine and interpret the environment from a variety of perspectives – physical, geographical, biological, sociological, economic, political, technological, historical, aesthetic, ethical and spiritual;
- arouse pupils' awareness and curiosity about the environment and encourage active participation in resolving environmental problems.

(From the Prospectus for the Conference on Education about the Environment, DfEE/DOE, February 1995)

---

* The booklet refers throughout to 'schools', although it is also relevant to the work of colleges.

To achieve these aims, schools can provide opportunities for learning **about, in, through** and **for** the environment.

- Education **about** the environment involves developing the sound base of knowledge, understanding and skills that pupils will need if they are to make sense of environmental issues.
- First-hand experience, or education **in** the environment, plays an essential part in learning. The experience can start in the school itself, in its grounds and immediate locality, progressing to activities in more distant, contrasting localities. The environment, at first-hand and through secondary sources, also provides a stimulus for learning a wide range of skills – education **through** the environment.
- Education **for** the environment involves developing informed concern about, and encouraging sensitive use of, the environment now and in the future. The focus is on sustainable solutions to environmental problems, taking into account the fact that there are conflicting interests and different perspectives, and informing the choices that we all have to make.

Although these distinctions help to clarify the scope of work on the environment, the phrase '**education about the environment**' is used throughout this booklet to embrace all curricular approaches.

THE NATIONAL CONTEXT

Education about the environment already takes place in all schools. Recent developments clarify the context within which that education takes place.

- The **National Curriculum subject Orders** require teaching about environmental matters. The original subject Orders were complemented by the National Curriculum Council's curriculum guidance on environmental education (NCC, 1990).
- **The Government is committed to environmental education** through Agenda 21, the international programme of action, arising from the United Nations 1992 'Earth Summit' in Rio de Janeiro. There is a Government Panel on sustainable development and many local councils have introduced Local Agenda 21 initiatives.
- **Regulations and guidance about environmental aspects of school buildings and grounds** from the Department for Education and Employment's Architects and Buildings Division advise on resource and energy management.
- **Legislation about the environment** affects schools; for example, the 1990 Environmental Protection Act requires school grounds to be kept litter free.
- Numerous **environmental organisations and initiatives** exist, some devised specifically for schools and many with direct Government support. Examples include 'Going for Green' (with its Eco-Schools initiative), Learning Through Landscapes, and Groundwork Trusts. (Contact details are given on page 11.)

SCOPE AND PURPOSE

The curriculum of all maintained schools must incorporate the National Curriculum subjects and religious education within the framework of the 1988 Education Reform Act. The reduced content and prescription of the 1995 revised subject Orders give schools greater freedom and flexibility to develop a curriculum that best meets the needs of their pupils.

It is for schools to decide how to teach environmental matters through the National Curriculum and how far to go beyond statutory obligations.

In some National Curriculum subjects, notably geography and science, the programmes of study ensure that environmental matters are taught. The geography Order, for example, requires that pupils study how sustainable development, stewardship and conservation considerations affect environmental planning and management. Similarly, the science Order requires study of life processes and living things.

Environmental matters may also feature in other National Curriculum subjects, not because they are required, but because schools choose to take up opportunities to include an environmental dimension.

The environment can also provide stimulating contexts for pupils, for example to learn how to take different views into account, cite evidence and construct persuasive arguments in English and develop and apply skills in information technology (IT) and mathematics.

Detailed National Curriculum requirements and opportunities for education about the environment are set out subject by subject in Section 3.

In many schools, education about the environment is supplemented by off-site and outdoor curricular activities and by personal and social education programmes. Some degree of coordination can prevent duplication of effort and help pupils to see the links between different parts of their work.

Other areas of school life, including those listed below, may also make an important contribution.

- The **school's approach to its own environment**, including care of the school buildings and grounds, energy efficiency, recycling, conservation, purchasing policy, use of materials and resources, and waste disposal.
- **Extra-curricular activities**, perhaps involving school clubs or membership of national societies, such as wildlife societies.
- **Special events** with an environmental focus, such as a 'tree week' or 'why we need water', either initiated by the school itself or in response to an external initiative.
- **Participation in environmental award schemes**, such as the Eco-Schools initiative supported by the Department of the Environment, and the National School Grounds Day.
- **School links with the local community**, such as local community projects with Groundwork or the British Trust for Conservation Volunteers to improve the environment.

Pupils' learning is likely to be most effective where curriculum content is matched by the school's own environmental practices and where work in the classroom is complemented by the sort of activities listed above. Planned links with young people's experience outside school, for example in youth clubs, Scouts and Guides, and the Duke of Edinburgh's Award Scheme, are also likely to enhance their environmental education.

Further guidance on developing these other aspects of school life may be found in *Our World – Our Responsibility: Environmental Education – A Practical Guide*, produced by the Council for Environmental Education and the Royal Society for the Protection of Birds (1996).

MANAGEMENT ISSUES

Education about the environment is more likely to be successful when it features in a school's aims, policies and development plans, which, in turn, are implemented and monitored. In considering the place of education about the environment, a school will want to consider its curriculum priorities and the example it sets in managing its own resources and environment.

Policies and plans can then be designed which will make clear the contribution that education about the environment can make to the overall achievement of the school's aims.

If the school decides to develop and implement such policies and plans, it will need to consider what constitutes high quality education about the environment. Some of the key elements and characteristics are listed below.

KEY ELEMENTS	CHARACTERISTICS
A coherent programme	Work in different curriculum areas needs to be coordinated and planned to ensure progression within and between phases.
High quality teaching, making use of a range of approaches	Teaching approaches are needed which promote the knowledge, understanding and skills that will allow pupils to understand and weigh evidence in addressing environmental issues.
First-hand practical experience	First-hand practical experience, for example, the practical monitoring of energy use within the school, will help to consolidate knowledge and understanding gained in the classroom.
Consistency between what is taught and practised	The content of the curriculum needs to be reflected in the way the school is run.

Measures to improve energy efficiency, for example, help pupils to appreciate that their own actions at a small scale may contribute to the resolution of large-scale environmental issues. |
| **Links with the local community** | Links with people in local businesses and local government, for example, will enable pupils to appreciate more fully the significance of environmental matters in their own locality and further afield. |
| **Opportunities for fieldwork** | Investigations outside the classroom help pupils gain awareness of the environment and develop understanding of environmental issues.

Education about the environment is concerned with the human as well as the physical and the urban as well as rural. Work in the school grounds, the immediate locality of the school and further afield, in contrasting environments, greatly enhances learning about the environment. |

KEY ELEMENTS	CHARACTERISTICS
Work on issues at a range of scales	Understanding is improved where environmental issues are investigated at a range of scales. A study of local environmental issues, with which pupils can engage directly, will help them make sense of issues at regional, national and global scales.
A range of evidence and viewpoints	In studying environmental issues, pupils should develop an awareness that environmental issues are invariably complex, and their solution involves weighing environmental considerations, alongside social and economic factors. They should develop a respect for evidence, an informed and critical understanding of different views and values, and a growing realisation that choices are seldom clear-cut.

AN APPROACH TO MANAGING SCHOOL DEVELOPMENT

This booklet suggests a flexible approach to managing school development of education about the environment. The approach can be adapted to suit a school's particular circumstances.

Managing curriculum development can be represented as a cyclical process with four main stages:

- audit;
- policy development and planning;
- implementation;
- evaluation and inspection.

Audit

An audit helps to determine the baseline or current level of activity.

An audit might include questions like:

- How is the school currently encouraging education about the environment?
- How does each curriculum area contribute?
- How is education about the environment managed and coordinated?
- What arrangements are there for work outside the classroom?
- To what extent are the the school grounds used as a learning resource?
- How is the use of the school grounds managed?
- How does the school monitor its use of resources?
- To what extent is there consistency between what is taught and practised?

Further guidance on audits may be found in *Towards a School Policy for Environmental Education: An Environmental Audit*, National Association for Environmental Education (UK), 1992.

Policy development and planning

Many schools have a written policy on environmental education, either as a free-standing document or as part of a wider curriculum statement.

A policy may specify:

- the aims, value and purpose of education about the environment in the school;
- the nature of pupils' entitlement;
- the way in which education about the environment is managed;
- external links, for example with Local Agenda 21 initiatives, and national environmental networks;
- guidance on health and safety issues;
- the way in which the school manages itself in a sustainable manner;
- information about how and by whom the policy was developed, the date of adoption by the governing body and the date of the next review;
- details about how the policy will be implemented and evaluated;
- a commitment to providing staff development for those involved;
- the relationship to other 'whole school' policies, for example those on work-related education and special educational needs.

A policy which is developed through consultation with all parties directly concerned (for instance teaching and non-teaching staff, governors, and pupils) is more likely to be implemented effectively.

Detailed guidance on developing a school environmental education policy and examples of policies may be found in a number of environmental education publications, for example *Our World – Our Responsibility: Environmental Education – A Practical Guide.*

Because of constraints of time and resources, most schools need to consider how changes can be prioritised and included in manageable steps within the school's overall development plan. Each priority may be broken down into specific targets.

For each target, a school could ask:

- What tasks need to be carried out?
- Who will be responsible for each task?
- By when does each task need to be completed?
- What standards need to be met?
- How will the work be resourced?
- How will success be judged?

Defining the tasks will involve decisions about aims, content, time allocation and structure. It will also involve choosing methods and approaches taking account of the particular needs of different groups of pupils. Specific support may be needed for some pupils, such as mid-term entrants, those for whom English is an additional language and pupils with special educational needs.

Implementation

Schools may adopt a wide range of implementation strategies. Whatever the detail, however, the arrangements need to be seen to have the full support of senior managers and the governing body.

Where a school decides to give an individual, or a group, responsibility for managing education about the environment, the tasks may include:

- promoting support for the programme;
- clarifying the relationship to other areas of the curriculum;
- clarifying staff roles and responsibilities;
- identifying staff development needs and organising training;
- securing the necessary physical and financial resources for implementation;
- assisting teachers in preparing schemes of work, developing materials and managing resources;
- working with teachers to develop links, to avoid undue overlap and plan progression, for example in the use of local sites by different year groups;
- supporting teaching and developing manageable arrangements for assessment and recording;
- working with local bodies, for example businesses, the planning department, and managers of sites used by the school.

Evaluation and inspection

Evaluation involves the gathering, analysis and interpretation of evidence about the quality of provision and its impact on pupils. The findings of evaluation can inform a school's decisions and support curriculum development.

Schools may wish to know the answers to a number of questions, for example:

- What have pupils gained from particular activities?
- Do individual pupils take part in a balanced and appropriate range of activities?
- Does the programme ensure progression in pupils' learning?
- Do **all** pupils have proper access to the programme?
- Is the school making the best use of time and other resources?
- How well do pupils use environmental resources provided in the school?
- Has the programme affected pupils' attitudes to, and behaviour in, the environment?
- Has the programme achieved its objectives – what succeeded, what failed and why?

A range of techniques may be used to answer these questions. Observation of lessons and other activities can provide evidence of learning and achievement. Questionnaires and interviews can be used for a variety of purposes, such as establishing the views of staff and pupils about the value of particular activities. The analysis of documentation such as policy statements and curriculum guidelines may also be helpful.

Education about the environment is not an explicit part of the OFSTED framework. However, an inspection may make judgements on the quality of a school's environment and on its work in promoting the spiritual, moral, cultural and social development of its pupils and preparing them for adult life. To the extent that a school's environmental policy and plans contribute to these aspects of school life, they will be reported on both directly and indirectly in an inspection. The quality of a school's partnership with the community is also evaluated.

Schools may, if they so wish, ask for their provision of education about the environment to be inspected as part of the overall inspection process.

FURTHER INFORMATION

There are many environmental organisations able to support environmental education in schools. The Council for Environmental Education (CEE) is the umbrella body for environmental education in England and Wales. The list below provides addresses and telephone numbers of environmental education organisations referred to in this booklet. A more comprehensive guide is provided in *Our World – Our Responsibility: Environmental Education – A Practical Guide,* produced by the Council for Environmental Education and the Royal Society for the Protection of Birds (1996).

Council for Environmental Education (CEE)
University of Reading, London Road, Reading RG1 5AQ. Tel. 01734 756061.
British Trust for Conservation Volunteers
36 St Mary's Street, Wallingford, Oxfordshire OX10 0EU. Tel. 01491 839766.
Centre for Research, Education and Training in Energy (CREATE)
Kenley House, 25 Bridgeman Terrace, Wigan WN1 1TD. Tel 01942 322271.
English Heritage
23 Savile Row, London W1X 1AB. Tel 0171 973 3000.
Field Studies Council
Preston Montford, Montford Bridge, Shrewsbury, Shropshire SY4 1HW. Tel 01743 850674
Going for Green
Churchgate House, 56 Oxford Street, Manchester M60 7HJ. Tel 0345 002100.
Groundwork Trust
85/87 Cornwall Street, Birmingham B3 3BY. Tel 0121 236 8565.
Learning Through Landscapes
3rd Floor, Southside Offices, The Law Courts, Winchester SO23 9DL. Tel 01962 846258.
National Association for Environmental Education
Wolverhampton University, Walsall Campus, Gorway Road, Walsall, West Midlands WS1 3BD. Tel 01922 31200.
Royal Society for the Protection of Birds
The Lodge, Sandy, Bedfordshire SG19 2DL. Tel 01767 680551.
Tidy Britain Group (Eco-Schools)
The Pier, Wigan WN3 4EX. Tel 01942 824620.
The Wildlife Trust
The Green, Witham Park, Waterside South, Lincoln LN5 7JR. Tel 01522 544400.
WWF-UK (World Wide Fund for Nature)
Panda House, Weyside Park, Godalming, Surrey GU7 1XR. Tel 01483 426444.

The examples in this section have been drawn from schools of different sizes and types in a range of environments throughout England and Wales. Each example illustrates how one or more of the key elements and characteristics described on pages 6 and 7 have contributed to the effectiveness of the teaching and learning about the environment.

Each example relates to National Curriculum requirements or opportunities. Some subject links are made explicit; in most cases, other opportunities can be inferred. The National Curriculum subject links in each may be considered further by reference to the appropriate subject requirements and opportunities listed in Section 3.

KEY STAGES 1 AND 2

EXAMPLE 1

A first school of about 240 pupils in a city in south west England	Development of school grounds to support teaching

Seven years ago, the school grounds consisted of a walled rectangle of tarmac. The grounds, of about half a hectare, now include small animals, a conservation area, a hide-and-seek garden, a rock garden, an assault course, a physical play area, a central area of grass, a Play Street, a covered area, two murals and a safe area for nursery children. At the front of the school is a recycling area shared with the local community. The school has worked closely with Learning Through Landscapes, the local council and commercial enterprises to bring about these changes.

The grounds are used to support the teaching of a number of subjects. Some examples are described below.

- **Science.** All areas of the grounds support investigative and experimental work, and health and safety considerations. Different parts of the grounds support particular activities. For example, the conservation area is used for habitat comparisons, classification (into plants and animals), and work on food chains.

- **Geography.** The grounds provide a rich locality study (physical and human features, similarities and differences, the weather, and how land is used) and opportunities to develop geographical skills, for example the use of geographical terms, following directions and making maps.

- **Design & technology.** The grounds have provided opportunities for designing and making (for example, a rabbit cage, a leaflet with a route walk for visitors, ways of keeping the hen house warm) and knowledge and understanding (for example, of the durability of different sorts of plant tubs).

- **Religious education.** The grounds provide pupils with the experience of nature's patterns and rhythms, including life and death. They are also used to prompt questions about the ethic of stewardship.

- **Music.** Sounds in the natural world, for example of the wind, rain and birds, are used as a starting point for compositions. Recordings of natural sounds are also used as a focus for the development of vocabulary to describe sounds.

KEY STAGE 1

EXAMPLE 2

| An infant school of around 265 pupils in a city in north west England | Surveying and redesigning school grounds |

The whole school was involved in surveying the original school grounds. All classes from nursery to Year 2 contributed to the findings of the survey by recording their observations and opinions.

The staff worked with a landscape consultant to design suitable investigations. Each class took responsibility for one of ten zones identified. The children worked from maps, architects' plans and their own observations to conduct a physical survey. They were involved in work on water, air, light and living things, each of which involved work in a number of National Curriculum subjects, especially **geography** and **science.**

Each class in the school then focused on a different aspect of design for the renewal of the school grounds. The nursery classes worked on designing a tricycle track, the reception classes designed different types of seating and miniature landscapes, and the Year 1 and 2 classes designed particular features, such as climbing frames, murals, a sensory garden, a food garden and shelters. The process provided a realistic context for a wide range of National Curriculum activities, notably in **design & technology, art** and **English.**

Children looked at examples of the features they were designing in parks and other schools. They talked to one another about their designs, drew them and made 3-D models of their final design, using clay, plasticine, construction kits or reclaimed materials. Children in each class presented their design ideas, through displays and assemblies, to the rest of the school.

The children's designs were shown to the landscape consultant, who used them, along with ideas from other members of the school community, to make a detailed plan for the development of the school grounds.

The children have since been involved in sending their designs to various organisations, inviting support for their construction. A number of positive responses have allowed the school to begin constructing parts of their renewed grounds.

KEY STAGE 1

Ideas from these children's design for a tricycle track were incorporated into the design of the one that was built

EXAMPLE 3

| A primary school of about 110 pupils in a village in eastern England | Using information technology in work on the environment |

The school grounds contain several different environmental study areas. These include conservation hedging around the perimeter, a variety of trees, an open water marsh, a large pond and a limestone mound. The areas have been designed to be used by children and teachers in all weather conditions. The school's work on its environmental areas provides a major context for its **information technology** (IT) provision in Key Stages 1 and 2. Conversely, as pupils' IT abilities develop, the use of IT enhances their environmental education.

In Key Stage 1, pupils are taught to use simple painting software to produce pictures. In Key Stage 2, they are taught to handle a more sophisticated range of hardware and software packages, which include video, desktop publishing, and the storage and retrieval of digitised images from videos. They choose the hardware and software appropriate to the task.

Pupils produce detailed observations on a monthly basis of aspects of the environmental areas, which are then communicated to other children and teachers in the school. Teachers use this information to plan work for their classes and may request additional information from the older children to further enhance their classroom activities. The documents produced by Year 6 pupils, which are stored in the school reference library, represent a developing account of the school environment.

The school environmental areas are also used extensively in developing pupils' knowledge, understanding and skills in **English**, **mathematics** and **science**. The school has documented the aspects of the programmes of study in each subject that can be developed through work linked to the environmental studies areas.

KEY STAGES 1 AND 2

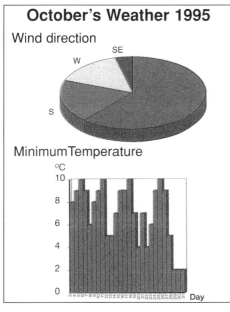

Information technology is used to record and display weather observations

A digitised image of an oak leaf retrieved from video

EXAMPLE 4

A primary school for pupils with severe learning difficulties in outer London.

Creating a nature trail in a woodland area

The school is situated in large grounds which include approximately one hectare of woodland. For many years, the woodland area had been impenetrable due to the extent of the undergrowth. A major project was undertaken to clear a pathway through the woods and make the area accessible for all children, including those in buggies and wheelchairs. The woodland now has several solid paths leading through it, a 'nature cabin' containing working and viewing areas, a large pond with a viewing platform to allow access for wheelchairs, and several bird feeding stations and nesting boxes.

Some of the aspects of the National Curriculum which are taught through the use of the nature trail are described below.

KEY STAGES 1 AND 2

Art   The nature trail provides a year-round stimulation for art activities. These range from simple bark rubbings to the creation of collages and displays incorporating items collected from the trail.

Science   A project on 'Living Things' draws heavily on the opportunities afforded by the nature trail. Pupils observe squirrels and birds from inside the nature cabin, collect a range of 'mini-beasts', which they look at through junior microscopes – before returning them to their environment – and, over a series of weeks, follow the development of the many tadpoles in the pond.

Physical Education   The nature trail provides a safe and stimulating environment for orienteering activities for pupils, in which pupils choose routes and follow markers along the trail to arrive at a predetermined spot.

Part of the school's nature trail

16

EXAMPLE 5

A rural primary school of about 270 pupils in northern England	Teaching about sustainable management in local woodland

The school has been developing its grounds for educational and leisure use over several years. It has recently begun to use a previously inaccessible woodland area to demonstrate sustainable woodland management.

The principal focus of the work was the National Curriculum Key Stage 2 **geography** requirement to look at how and why people seek to manage and sustain their environment, but the work opened up many other opportunities for teaching aspects of other subjects in both Key Stages 1 and 2.

The mainly oak woodland had been unmanaged for many years. Some of the trees were degenerating and the denseness of the growth meant that there was little regeneration or variety of plant growth which would have made it a rich habitat. It was a microcosm of a problem facing the area as a whole, where most of the woodlands were planted at the same time and, after years of neglect, are coming to the end of their lifespan. Local coppicers pruned dead wood and sideshoots, improving the health of the trees and letting in light to allow for natural regeneration. Pupils then helped the coppicers to strip the bark from the branches and traditional methods were used to make a small fenced area in the wood, in which staff and children can work.

Another class was studying tropical rainforests at the time this was happening and links were made, stressing sustainable management of forests.

Subsequent work using the area of woodland has included:

- a study by Year 2 children of the 'mini-beasts' found in the wood – KS1 **science** (life processes and living things) and KS1 **mathematics** (handling data);
- a litter survey – KS1 **geography** and KS1 **mathematics** (number);
- sculpture work using natural materials – KS2 **art**;
- children writing poems about the environment – KS2 **English** (writing).

KEY STAGES 1 AND 2

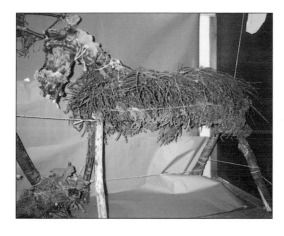

An animal sculpture using natural materials

EXAMPLE 6	
A primary school of about 280 pupils in inner London	Teaching about the built environment

As part of an English Heritage pilot scheme 'Schools Adopt Monuments', the school chose to adopt three local monuments: its own school building, a shop in a local street, and a hospital dating back to the eleventh century.

The overall aim of the work was to study in depth the built environment, social history and links between the school and the local community. The work provided opportunities for work in a number of National Curriculum subjects, notably **history** and **art.**

The pupils drew plans, built models and undertook measuring and estimating activities. They used a wide variety of documentary evidence, photographs, video recordings and oral histories. Several visits were undertaken. The pupils created designs for new windows for the chapel in the hospital, and built up strong links with the patients.

KEY STAGES 1 AND 2

During the work, pupils wrote letters and designed invitations, information sheets and programmes. They carried out interviews and had articles published in the local press.

EXAMPLE 7	
A primary school of about 100 pupils in a village in Wales	Linking teaching and learning with concern for the environment

Environmental work has been given a high profile within the school for a number of years. The school grounds have been improved through tree and hedge planting. Litter sweeps of the school have widened to include the village. Areas around the village, including pathways and river banks, have also been cleared with assistance from the Tidy Britain Group. The school, with help from governors, parents, children and teachers, has also developed a wetland conservation area.

The school has a committee comprising staff, governors and children, to coordinate environmental education in the school. All schemes of work are planned with an environmental aspect involved. Work in a range of subjects has an environmental focus. In **design & technology,** for example, children have designed and made signs and created a working windmill.

Recently, the school has also introduced an environmental dimension into the conduct of its own affairs by trying to cut waste through recycling and reducing fuel consumption. The school has registered as an Eco-School and has won a 'Green Flag' award.

EXAMPLE 8

Four schools – two first schools, a primary and a middle school – with a total of about 1000 pupils, located on a single campus in a suburb of a city in northern England

Studying local environmental issues – traffic and road safety

Local people were concerned about road safety and traffic. A local architecture workshop was asked to work with the four schools to develop a joint strategy to deal with the problems.

Pupils in a Year 6 class devised a short questionnaire on the subject of journeys to and from school. They identified a 20 per cent sample from the school roll and conducted the questionnaire with this sample. The pupils analysed the survey results, identifying problems and discussing possible solutions.

The teacher integrated the theme of journeys to and from school into a study with a **geography** focus of the pupils' locality. The teacher used the project to teach aspects of other National Curriculum subjects.

History: questioning parents and grandparents to discover how journeys to school have changed; studying changes in transport in the local area since 1930, using old maps and photographs.

Mathematics: collecting, presenting and analysing data on pupils' journeys to school; conducting traffic counts at different times; calculating speed, time and distance.

Science: assessing dust levels and measuring sound levels at locations around the school at different times, looking for patterns in the data collected and suggesting reasons for them.

KEY STAGES
1 AND 2

Left: Year 6 pupils measuring sound levels on the nearby main road

The teacher of a Year 1/2 class integrated the project into work on the school and its locality. The children made mental maps of their journey to school on a particular day and identified problems they experienced. These were depicted in pictures and writing.

The project led to a display of children's work in the local library. Parents from all four schools then met with local councillors, officers from the Highway Authority and the police to decide how to alleviate the problem. Some of the solutions suggested by pupils and parents are already in place. This approach is being considered as a model to use with other schools in the city as it illustrates the practice of consulting young people about local issues.

**KEY STAGES
1 AND 2**

One Year 2 pupil's view of the problems and solutions

Another Year 2 pupil's map of her journey to school

EXAMPLE 9

| A primary school of about 130 pupils in a village which has become a suburb of a midlands town | Studying local environmental issues – a plan for a new road |

The school, which faces directly on to a main road, is near the route for a planned new road which would bypass the village. The new road will bring some environmental benefits, for example a reduction in traffic in the village, but will also have detrimental effects on the environment along its route.

A Year 6 unit of work, with a **geography** focus, was planned to investigate the implications of the scheme and to consider how the change could be managed to sustain, rather than diminish, the quality of life of the village residents. As well as developing geographical and other skills, the study developed pupils' knowledge and understanding of settlement, environmental change, and the locality of the school. The investigation focused on a number of questions:

- Why is the road needed?
- What is the planned route for the road?
- What are the different points of view about the development?
- Who is involved in making the decision?
- How will the environment be affected?

KEY STAGE 2

Pupils carried out their own surveys, for example a traffic survey and a survey of residents' opinions, which revealed a wide range of different views on the bypass. The pupils compared their results with those of the local planning authority. A local planner visited the school and talked to the pupils about the scheme. Pupils were able to consider different opinions on the issue before forming their own view. They also began to appreciate how the planning process works and the role of individuals in it.

A pupil's account of what people think about the new road

EXAMPLE 10

| A primary school of about 250 pupils in inner London | Working with an urban studies centre on local environmental issues |

This Year 6 **geography** unit of work was run in collaboration with a local urban studies centre, as part of the launch of the local council's Local Agenda 21 initiative. The work offered opportunities for pupils to develop geographical skills while learning about the locality of their school and environmental change.

Pupils explored reasons for some of the problems in their local environment and how they could be addressed. Over four half-day sessions, the pupils learned about the purposes of Agenda 21 and the types of issues the local initiative could tackle. They created an exhibition to raise public awareness of the initiative.

The work focused on a number of questions:

- What are the good and bad features of our local environment?
- How do the features affect different people?
- What do different people think about them?
- How can the environment be maintained or improved?
- What can we do to help?

The pupils took photographs of attractive and unattractive features of the school's locality. They also wrote about the features, bearing in mind the questions being addressed.

KEY STAGE 2

One pupil's view about a local playground

It is good because it is a place for children to play. It is bad because: no one looks after it; there used to be a slide and some swings but they have been taken away. Because there is no padding on the floor the people who take their children to the play-ground must hold the child so they can't relax. There are no benches to sit on. All the lights have been broken or graffitti has been sprayed on them. I think the walls should be repainted once in a while. A slope should be made and more care should be taken over it in general. Guardians of the children must constantly look at their children to make sure their child is alright. The council could change the play ground by making it safer and by putting more play things in. Local people could help by raising money to improve the play ground.

A number of people involved in environmental improvement were invited to the school. They included representatives of environmental groups and officers from the local council. The children interviewed them about their roles in solving environmental problems, asking questions that they had prepared in advance.

An exhibition of the pupils' work was displayed at the Local Agenda 21 launch, which was attended by people from local groups and organisations. Some pupils attended to present and explain their work.

This was a short and manageable project which built on the pupils' general local environmental knowledge and helped them to understand how they can contribute to environmental improvement, both through their own actions and by influencing others.

> This road affects pedestrians because it can affect their hearing and their breathing, (health). People who drive down this road will have a different opinion about the road than pedestrians. I think council and government can ask scientists to design electric cars. Another idea is that government can make public transport cheap and more efficient.

Another pupil's views about a main road

EXAMPLE 11

| A primary school in a village in northern England | Work with a geography focus as part of a Local Agenda 21 Initiative |

The school was invited by a National Park Planning Board to involve its pupils in planning the future development of the village. Year 6 pupils contributed to the parish council's 'village scheme' by producing a photographic record of what they thought were positive and negative features of the village environment, mapping changes, investigating traffic congestion and interviewing local people about footpath access around the village.

Pupils developed their geographical skills by investigating environmental change in the school locality. The work also provided a context for work in **English**. Pupils practised and developed their writing – for example, by drafting, revising and presenting a written report to the National Park Officer – and their speaking and listening – for example, by interviewing a number of adults, including the National Park ranger, members of the parish council, the local MP and members of the Board of the National Park.

The results of the pupils' work were displayed in the village. The pupils also wrote to the National Park Officer about their concerns. As a result the National Park planning department agreed to include the protection of the 'conker' tree in the village development brief.

The link to 'Agenda 21' gave the work added value by emphasising environmental futures, consultation, liaison with decision-makers and sustainability.

EXAMPLE 1 2

| A primary school of about 210 pupils in a town in south east England | Teaching about a controversial environmental issue |

The Sea Empress oil spill off the Pembrokeshire coast was studied by a Year 5 class. The study provided opportunities for work in a number of subjects, notably **English, geography** and **science.**

Pupils had seen news of the incident on television and were worried by it. The teacher developed their awareness through discussion, factual report-writing about the event, and writing about the feelings it engendered. Information was gathered from newspaper articles and through considering the various viewpoints the teacher and pupils had heard expressed on television.

The teacher was aware of the risk, in studying controversial issues, of exploiting pupils' trust in their teacher's opinion and was concerned about possible parental reponses to children's interpretation of what has been said in school. She therefore ensured that pupils were made aware of different views on where responsibility for the spill lay and what should be done to prevent similar incidents occurring in the future. Pupils also considered the issue within the wider context of our need for oil and oil products.

Materials were provided from a variety of sources and the teacher often played 'devil's advocate' by putting alternative viewpoints to those expressed in the materials or by pupils. The teacher helped pupils to read critically by drawing attention to the use of sensational headlines and balancing them with information about the limited long-term effects of the Shetland oil spill five years earlier.

EXAMPLE 1 3

| Two schools in the midlands, one a junior school of about 350 pupils, the other a primary school of about 165 pupils, and a field studies centre in eastern England | Practical studies of energy conservation |

Both schools have developed units of work to study heat and heating, types of fuel, shelter and comfort, buildings, recycling and looking after the environment. The work builds on aspects of the National Curriculum programmes of study for **science, mathematics, design & technology, geography** and **Information Technology**. Specific references to energy have been removed from the Key Stage 2 Programmes of Study for science and geography, but both schools have chosen to retain the topic in their teaching programmes.

KEY STAGE 2

A Year 4 class in one of the schools carried out a study of energy conservation in cooperation with the district council. The council gave the school leaflets and information about energy efficiency and provided a vacant bungalow for the children to use for the day to explore energy efficiency.

Pupils then applied their knowledge and understanding to a study of energy efficiency in the school, which provided many opportunities for teaching aspects of the National Curriculum. For example, surveying warm and cold areas of the school involved the use of thermometers, while considering heat loss through doors and windows helped pupils to learn about area, plan drawing and the need for accuracy in measurement. The creation of a database to store the data for subsequent analysis encouraged the development of information technology skills.

The school created an 'E-Team' to build on and sustain the pupils' awareness of energy efficiency. The E-Team is a group of children who take responsibility for monitoring and policing the use and wastage of energy in school. E-Team members meet regularly with a teacher coordinator and representatives provide feedback to their own classes. Their responsibilities include reducing energy usage and cost by, for example, switching off unwanted lights. Interest is maintained by the regular introduction of new projects, such as can recycling and Christmas card collection.

The school has also established links with people from local and national industry, the Centre for Research, Education and Training in Energy (CREATE), and the local Training and Enterprise Council (TEC).

KEY STAGE 2

In the second school, pupils' work on energy in **science** was linked to a school project to reduce the school's energy costs. Working with the Fuel Economy Officer from the local council, the school embarked on a programme to monitor fuel consumption. Pupils carried out a survey of 'energy awareness' among all concerned in the life of the school. This led to the adoption of good energy housekeeping measures in the school, a system of pupil energy monitors, and a regular update on progress to all in the school.

Not only did the project provide a real-life context for the pupils' studies, but it also helped the school to achieve a 24 per cent saving in its energy costs over two years.

The field studies centre also aimed to reduce its per capita consumption of energy and to encourage users of the centre to reduce their energy and resource consumption. Use of energy and resources is monitored on a regular basis. Separate meters have been installed in the centre's various buildings to allow energy consumption in each to be monitored separately. Weekly readings are transferred to a computer spreadsheet, which calculates per capita consumption and produces graphs of the results.

During their visits, pupils are made aware of the need to conserve resources by a combination of teaching activities, graphical displays of resource use, and the direct involvement of visiting groups in the monitoring process.

EXAMPLE 14

A small primary school in a town in northern England

Assessing environmental quality: rivers and pollution

A group of Year 5/6 pupils carried out an investigation of a local river to explore its effects on the landscape, the effects of human activity, and how the river may be managed and sustained. In addition to its main focus on **geography**, the study also contributed to the pupils' work in **science** on life processes and living things, and provided opportunities to develop a wide range of skills in these and other subjects.

Because of the school's location, the work was given added meaning by setting it within the wider context of the Mersey Basin Campaign, an environmental improvement campaign supported by the Department of the Environment and industrial and commercial organisations.

Pupils studied past use of the river, when local cotton mills were powered by river water. They learned that the river was heavily polluted in the past by bleach and dye works and that pollution remains an issue today. As the school is located near the confluence of two rivers, a comparative study with a cleaner river was carried out. Fieldwork played an important part in the work, but the nature of the fieldwork was determined by health and safety considerations, which themselves are influenced by water quality. In planning the work, the school used materials from the Mersey Basin Campaign, which included guidance on health and safety considerations, and the Wildlife Trust's *River Watch* pack.

For the more polluted river, visual assessments of pollution were made, for example a litter count, a visual assessment of detergent foam on the water, and an assessment of the colour of the water. In the cleaner river, 'dipping' was used to determine water quality, by the collection of indicator species.

Having investigated the issue for themselves, pupils considered other evidence, in the form of extracts from local newspapers. They also considered ways in which an environmental improvement project could be carried out in their local river.

EXAMPLE 15

A middle school of about 800 pupils in a small town in south west England

Linking work on a local threatened environment with a global issue

Each year group in this middle school studies one topic which raises a global environmental issue through a local environment visited by all pupils. Year 6 pupils, for example, study the dangers for the local peat moors of extraction and flooding, and the effects of intensive agriculture.

The study incorporates work on environmental change in **geography**, it also covers life processes and living things, and materials and their properties in **science**. It involves the development of a range of geographical and scientific skills. Economic and industrial understanding is also encouraged by, for example, an activity considering the effect of using environmentally friendly materials on the prices of products.

All pupils visit a local nature reserve, where they compare the biodiversity of the peat moor with the agricultural monocultures on the edge of the moors. They also visit an Iron Age Centre, where, for example, they make wattle and daub and burn charcoal. Detailed first-hand study of bog plants and insects is carried out in the school grounds, where a pond has been silted up to create a bog.

The work is carried out during seven periods a week taught by the form tutor. The emphasis is on science and geography but aspects of **mathematics**, **English** and **information technology** are also developed. The planning of the topics is overseen by a curriculum team which includes the heads of science and geography, and the head of lower school. This team briefs the form tutors. Members of staff from other subjects are consulted when relevant.

The classroom and fieldwork activities take place within an overall school framework that gives high priority to environmental education. For example, the school ensures that biodiversity in the school grounds is built into the school development plan. Each pupil also has a 'green book' in which they keep a record of their classroom work.

KEY STAGE 2

EXAMPLE 16	
A primary school of about 150 pupils in the centre of a city in northern England	A study of a local town square

This work was carried out by the school – in conjunction with a local architecture workshop – as part of an international project on town squares. The school became involved because of its location on the edge of a Georgian town square close to the city centre. The square, which was once part of a highly desirable residential area, has gone through a period of decline, but has now been designated a conservation area.

A class of pupils in Years 5 and 6 carried out a study of the square for their local **history** study unit. Children's awareness of the buildings in the locality was increased by, for example the drawing of maps and annotated sketches. Pupils investigated the history of the square and visited the County Archive and the Central Library to study primary materials and discover the history behind the buildings in the square. The education officer from the architecture workshop supported the class teacher throughout.

The children produced a town trail of the square as a resource for the school. Other local schools have also been informed of the resource. A book of children's work was produced and sent to a twin school in Sweden, which responded with a book from its pupils who had been doing similar work in their locality. The work is to be exhibited at an international exhibition of children's work on town squares.

ACROSS KEY STAGES

EXAMPLE 17

A day/residential school in the midlands for pupils with physical disabilities, who may have associated learning difficulties, speech and hearing difficulties, emotional difficulties, or visual impairment. The school has just over 100 pupils in the 2 to 18+ age range

Learning out of the classroom

**ACROSS
KEY STAGES**

The school uses its environmental policy not only to enrich the curriculum, including its teaching of the National Curriculum, but also more specifically, to present a series of learning challenges appropriate to each pupil's physical and mental capabilities. Every opportunity is taken to teach pupils outside the classroom.

Pupils visit a nearby field centre managed by the local power station; the grounds have been specially adapted for wheelchairs and for pupils with mobility problems. Exercises in pond dipping, leading to identification and classification (**science**: life processes and living things) are the main activities, but the vocabulary enrichment and the general development of language are equally important (**English**: speaking and listening).

A group of pupils has also planned improvements to the surrounds of the school pond which is accessible to pupils in wheelchairs. This detailed surveying project, conducted by pupils, involved work in **mathematics** (shape, space and measures) and on the use of materials in **design & technology.**

Counting ladybirds in the centre's grounds

Follow-up work in the centre's classroom

EXAMPLE 18

An upper school in a town in eastern England and ten associated middle and primary schools	A special event on environmental issues and sustainability

This week-long event was planned by an upper school and its associated middle and primary schools. Its aims included increased awareness and understanding of sustainable development and local and global environmental issues.

A large exhibition at the upper school covered issues relating to sustainable development, for example: endangered species and disappearing habitats; poverty; water; environmental health; world food and farming; energy; pollution; local conservation; trade and aid; the debt crisis; and world population.

Hundreds of pupils in the middle and primary schools visited the exhibition and were involved in a wide range of activities relating to work in different subjects. The activities included work on litter, waste and recycling, energy efficiency, tropical rainforests, local conservation issues and pollution problems. At the entrance of the exhibition, visitors were welcomed by the sights and sounds of a tropical rainforest, which were developed, as part of a curriculum liaison project, by primary, middle and upper school pupils.

All pupils in the upper school attended workshops run by visiting experts on local and global issues. These related to the areas covered in the exhibition and to specific curriculum work, for example in **geography**, **science**, **information technology**, **art** and **music**. An exhibition and workshops about renewable energy and energy conservation, for example, were related to work in science and information technology.

Many parents also visited the main exhibition and came to a production of the musical 'Yanomamo' about life in rainforests, performed by pupils from the middle and upper schools as part of a music and liaison project between the schools.

A key feature of the event, and one of importance in the local Agenda 21 process, was partnership between the schools, the local education authority, the local council and the local Wildlife Trust.

ACROSS
KEY STAGES

EXAMPLE 19

An environmental education centre in south east England, catering for pupils aged 4–18, including pupils from special schools	Linking work on the environment with information technology

The centre is set in eight hectares of varied habitat, which include two hectares of freshwater lake and part of a river. Visiting pupils have access to a full range of practical work, supported by extensive research data accumulated at the centre. Programmes relating to all National Curriculum subjects are offered. The centre is jointly operated by the county council and a national power company.

The centre is developing links between environmental education activities, notably in **geography** and **science**, and **information technology.** Visiting pupils have opportunities to measure and record physical characteristics, such as the oxygen, nitrate and temperature levels, of the centre's lakes. They can contribute to the biological database, which, for twenty years, has monitored the biodiversity of species, or record and interpret weather data from the centre's automatic weather station.

ACROSS KEY STAGES

The centre has a presence on the Internet, which enables pupils to exchange information relating to their studies, for example seasonal variations of populations of freshwater invertebrates.

Pupils working with a video microscope, which is capable of showing the structure of cells, are able to view and examine living specimens at very high magnification. They are then able to record the images either as video clips or stills, which are digitised and can be stored in a computer database. These images can then be retrieved for further study or printed out as hard copy in full colour. Pupils are able to take images or video records back to school with them for further study on, for example, the adaptation of organisms to life in fresh water.

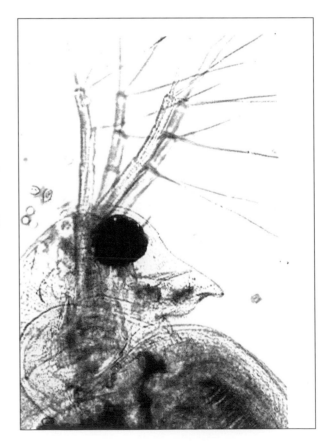

A digitised magnified image of the head of a Daphnia

KEY STAGES 3 AND 4

EXAMPLE 20

A middle school of about 800 pupils in a small town in south west England

A study of resources, energy and the landscape

This Year 8 study looks at the effects of extractive industries on the landscape. It links a study of open-cast mining in the Vale of Belvoir with the quarrying of limestone locally. The pupils are taught about the local quarrying industry, with the help of a video made by members of staff who had industrial placements with the local limestone quarrying company. Pupils also explore the potential of alternative ways of generating power, using the school's 'sustainability laboratory', which contains, for example, a model of the national grid, windmills and a working hydro-electric model. The pupils discover, through a 'child-power' generator, the importance of conserving energy. They are also taught about the national distribution of quarrying and mining. Pupils then investigate three alternative futures – no change (with the current problems they have explored), investment in nuclear power (involving the building of a further nuclear power station locally), or investment in renewable energy sources (involving building a wind farm on a nearby hill, thereby spoiling an area of scenic attraction).

During the course of the study, all pupils visit the local nuclear power station. There is also an additional optional three-day trip to Wales to visit the Centre for Alternative Technology, the Vale of Rheidol hydro-power station and a wind farm.

The study involves work in **geography**, on economic activities and environmental issues, and **science**, on physical processes, and materials and their properties. It also provides opportunities for the development of a wide range of skills in geography, science and other National Curriculum subjects.

Science and geography teachers teach the necessary facts and concepts, while form tutors explore the importance of values and attitudes as part of the **personal and social education** curriculum.

KEY STAGE 3

EXAMPLE 21

A secondary school of about 650 pupils in a town in northern England | Fieldwork involving a number of subjects

The school builds into its teaching programme a number of cross-subject environmental activities. Each year, for example, all Year 7 pupils from the school take part in a day's fieldwork at Flamborough Head. A number of subject departments – **mathematics**, **English**, **science**, **design & technology**, **geography** and **art** – participate, with the aim of integrating the environment into their schemes of work. The day is planned to ensure that the exercise is coherent and meets the learning objectives of each subject.

Pupils are divided into groups and take part in a cycle of activities illustrating a variety of ways in which the environment can be investigated. The activities include building a survival shelter, surveying, map reading and field sketching. After the visit, the work is followed up in each subject.

KEY STAGE 3

Mathematics – pupils read off their own slope measurements

Art – landscape sketching

Art – the final product

- In **mathematics**, pupils write up the results of their surveying, produce scale drawings and, in collaboration with the design & technology department, produce a scale model of the bay.
- In **geography**, pupils write word-processed fieldwork reports, including field sketches and sketch maps, as part of a unit of study on coasts.
- In **science**, pupils produce labelled transects of a wave-cut platform, showing zones of plant and animal life. Other findings are integrated into work on the rock cycle and food chains.

The exercise is evaluated each year by teachers of the subjects involved.

Subject links identified by the departments involved

MATHEMATICS

Using & applying mathematics
1a, 2ac, 3abc

Number
1ab, 3c

Shape space & measure
1b, 2bd, 3d

SCIENCE

Experimental & Investigative
1g   fieldwork
2   obtaining evidence
3   analysing evidence & drawing conclusions

Living things in their environment
5ab   adaptation
5cd   feeding relationships
5fg   competition

Materials & their properties
2fgh geological changes

ENGLISH

Writing
1ab   writing for a range of purposes and audiences
2b   developing pupils' ability to write poetry

KEY STAGE 3

Flamborough Head Environmental Education Year 7 cross-subject fieldwork: links to programmes of study

---

INFORMATION TECHNOLOGY

2b communicate information, for example in geography and English

---

DESIGN & TECHNOLOGY

1b   design & technology capability through focused practical tasks
2a   work in teams
2b   apply skills from other subjects
3   designing skills
4   making skills

GEOGRAPHY

2b   investigate theme
3a   geographical vocabulary
3b   fieldwork
3d   using maps
8c   geomorphological processes – coasts
15a   environmental issues – conflict in areas of scenic attraction

---

ART

2b   record observations
4abcd   visual elements
6   practical use of materials
7a   record responses to environment
7b   gather resources and materials

EXAMPLE 22	
A secondary school of about 1200 pupils in a city in north west England	Developing environmental work across subjects

The school, which is involved in the World Wide Fund for Nature's Curriculum Management Scheme, is devising ways to develop environmental work across the curriculum. Each faculty has a coordinator, whose role is to monitor and develop environmental work within the faculty.

In a Year 8 unit of work in **religious education,** for example, pupils undertake work on Christianity and the environment, during which they learn about Christian ideas and attitudes to stewardship of the world's resources.

Similarly, in **mathematics,** time is set aside in Year 8 for mathematical work with an environmental theme. Some pupils practise their number skills by investigating the benefits of recycling or how energy conservation measures in the home can reduce carbon dioxide production, while others develop their data handling skills in investigations of movements of goods by different types of transport in Britain.

A coherent programme of environmental education within the curriculum is central to the school's commitment to education for sustainability. Other approaches are also being employed. Pupils are encouraged to participate in decision-making processes through a range of consultative groups, including an active school council, year councils, and a canteen group, which has managed to reinstate re-usable cutlery after the contractors introduced disposable cutlery.

A 'Green Group' comprising volunteer pupils has organised paper and can recycling facilities for the school and local community. Half of the money raised is used for activities decided by the Green Group. These have included the provision of additional paper and can collection points. Members of the Green Group sit on the school council and contribute to policy decisions. The group's activities fit within the school development plan.

'Focus fortnights', assemblies, displays and **personal and social education** are also used to develop understanding of sustainable development.

EXAMPLE 23

| Two secondary schools, one of about 1550 pupils in a town in south west England, the other of about 850 pupils in a midlands city | Geographical approaches to global issues |

A six-week module in one school's Year 8 **geography** course provides opportunities for pupils to develop their geographical skills through one of their studies of a country. The module includes work on ecosystems and development, and raises the issue of the future of the rainforests.

The department has developed an approach which is differentiated according to the abilities of the pupils. Able pupils are given an open-ended task with a prompt sheet which suggests what they should aim to achieve at various stages of the project. Lower attaining pupils are given worksheets listing the things they need to find out and suggesting where they might find the information.

Pupils use a range of resources in the school, including computer software, CDs and video material. They also write to environmental organisations to gather further information. The module includes a visit to the local zoo, where they can see rainforest plants and animals at first hand in the tropical house. The project concludes with a debate, for which pupils are given role cards and have to use information from their research to prepare and present their case.

In the second school, a Year 10 GCSE **geography** module on development has been revised to strengthen understanding of the need for sustainable development, with the aims of challenging accepted definitions of development and promoting exploration of attitudes.

The key question for the module is 'what is development?' and, in the first session, pupils sort a set of cards about the meaning of development. A range of information is introduced during the course of the unit, including statistical data about gross national product (GNP), birth rates, infant mortality and life expectancy, video material showing family lifestyles in four countries in different states of development, and development indices from several different sources. All pupils keep a record book, in which they record their ideas and opinions after analysing each new set of information.

The pupils' definitions of development change during the process. One pupil's definition changed from 'improvement in, for example, medicine and technology' to 'everyone having the resources they need for survival', while another's definition changed from 'when a place is being modernised' to 'people's lives becoming better'.

**KEY STAGES
3 AND 4**

EXAMPLE 24

Two secondary schools, one of about 650 pupils on the edge of a town in northern England, the other of about 1350 girls in inner London

Developing school grounds to support teaching

Despite their contrasting situations, both schools have developed their school grounds for teaching purposes. The school in northern England has, for a number of years, successfully involved pupils in the development and use of the school environment. The aims have been:

● to improve the quality and diversity of the habitats of the school site so that they are more attractive to and supportive of local wildlife;

● to involve pupils in the general improvement of their own environment so that they feel ownership of and responsibility for their own surroundings.

The school's environment group, involving both pupils and staff, is responsible for the development and management of the habitats, each of which must be sustainable and of use as a study resource. The school now provides opportunities for pupils to study, at first hand, pond, wetland, woodland, scrubland, limestone cliff, hedgerow and open grassland habitats.

The opportunities for **science** teaching throughout the school provided by these various habitats include: identifying plants, birds and animals; developing skills of biological sampling, measurement and classification; laboratory and outdoor work on the growth and development of plants; and developing understanding of the interrelationships between plant and animal populations and communities.

The development of the school grounds, for which the school has won four awards since 1992, for example from the local water authority, has taken place in a school which gives a high priority to environmental matters. The school site contains can collection and recycling bins and is kept clean by regular litter patrols by each class.

The school in inner London has developed its less extensive grounds to include a nature trail, a woodland edge, a butterfly and bird garden, meadows, and various recycling bins. A number of subject departments, including **science**, **geography**, **design & technology** and **history**, are developing their use of the grounds for teaching purposes.

By using the grounds for teaching and a range of other activities, including a thriving 'Growing Club', a half-termly Science Environment Week, and regular Open Days for local primary school children to experience the site, a real attempt is made to involve pupils directly in planting and in taking care of the site, teaching sustainability, biodiversity and stewardship.

The school has involved a number of outside agencies, including Learning Through Landscapes, the British Trust for Conservation Volunteers, the local Environment Trust, a local university and a bank, in its environmental work.

Planting a Swedish whitebeam

EXAMPLE 25

| A secondary school of about 1350 pupils in a small town in south east England | Coordinating work on environmental education |

The school saw a need to coordinate environmental aspects of the revised National Curriculum. To improve coordination, the school responsibility structure has been reorganised. Departments have been regrouped as faculties. Each faculty has key stage leaders who work together to ensure that the coverage of cross-subject issues, such as environmental education, is comprehensive and integrated. They also have responsibility for progression between key stages.

A recent curriculum audit revealed a range of environmental topics in subject schemes of work, often duplicating work and rarely coordinated between departments. The environmental policy has been revised with the agreement of the heads of faculty and several initiatives have been agreed.

KEY STAGES 3 AND 4

- **Extending teaching about the environment across the curriculum.** For example:
  - **religious education**: a study of attitudes to the environment in different religions has been added to the scheme of work;
  - **modern foreign languages**: pupils on exchanges find out about attitudes to the environment in European schools. A group of pupils recently joined an international drama production about world environmental issues in the school's twinned German school;
  - **geography** and **science**: modification of schemes of work to coordinate the teaching of environmental topics in these subjects;
  - **personal and social education**: inclusion in form periods of topics raising awareness of the environment, which are linked to assembly themes for the week.

- **Involving pupils directly in improving their school environment.** The school student council has an environment committee, which advises on developments to the school grounds. Recent initiatives have included planting and landscaping of borders, a major tree planting scheme, improving signs and controlling traffic within the school. An annual fund-raising day generates money for these initiatives and involves the whole school in a ten-mile walk in the local countryside. All Year 7 pupils spend a follow-up day working on a variety of environmental projects sponsored by the farming community and relevant to the Key Stage 3 geography and science curricula.

- **Evaluating the effectiveness of environmental education**. The student record of achievement has been adapted to include evidence of coverage and understanding of environmental education and other cross-subject topics.

EXAMPLE 26

Two secondary schools, one of about 900 pupils in inner London, the other of about 1200 pupils in a small town in south east England	Raising awareness of environmental issues through special events

One school took part in a project for World Environment Day 1994. An exercise called 'Mapping the Future' was carried out across all year groups in the **English** department, with input from some **science** and **geography** classes. Pupils of all ages and abilities worked in small groups to research an environmental issue which they had chosen. They then made a presentation, in the form of poetry, reports, descriptions, transcribed interviews or imaginative writing, about possible futures.

In science and geography, groups of pupils researched chosen topics about the school's locality. These included noise pollution and possible uses for, and protection of, the green spaces in a local housing estate.

Pupils produced a high standard of work. Many pupils researched topics in their own time. The project engaged the interest of pupils, from the most able to those with special educational needs. A display of work by pupils of all ages and abilities was mounted in the foyer. This was seen by parents and governors, as well as journalists from two local papers. As a result of World Environment Day coverage, pupils from the school were interviewed for an article in a national newspaper and a group of Year 9 and 10 pupils recorded an interview on environmental matters for a national radio programme.

In the second school, Environment Weeks and bi-annual Special Conference Days give pupils opportunities to apply their knowledge and understanding of environmental matters learnt in the classroom to real-life situations.

One conference day gave pupils the opportunity to take a critical look at their local environment. Pupils explored issues such as the loss of local downland to road building, the increasing dereliction of the town centre caused by the development of out-of-town superstores, and pollution on local beaches caused by sewage dumping. The issues were explored through public surveys, debates and interviews with people involved or affected. During the event pupils made a video, which showed the connections between environmental issues and social, economic and political considerations.

The video was shown at the 1994 World Environment Day launch in London and, subsequently, excerpts were shown on the regional television news. The Chairman of the local water authority, who disputed the pupils' criticisms about levels of water pollution, visited the school to listen to the findings of the pupils and put his views about water quality in the area.

KEY STAGES 3 AND 4

EXAMPLE 27

A secondary school of about 1200 pupils in outer London	A whole-school approach to environmental education

The school has always placed great importance on environmental education. Staff decided that the school's environmental practices should match its teaching and that environmental work should:

● be linked to pupils' own lives;
● involve consideration of ways in which environmental problems may be tackled;
● focus on affective and emotional aspects as well as cognitive ones.

A working party, including the environmental education coordinator, a member of senior management and a teacher from each subject area, was set up to take an overview of environmental issues across the school. External funding from the World Wide Fund for Nature, over a two-year period, paid for supply cover so that staff could spend time on this work.

KEY STAGES 3 AND 4

An environmental issue is introduced into each year group's **personal and social education** course and understanding is developed by discussion, role play or individual written work. Connections are made between the issue and what pupils can do in their own lives.

Design & technology courses link design exercises to the solution of environmental problems. A GCSE project led to the design of a system in which a solar panel and wind generator powered a fountain, a waterfall and lights. A British Gas Award enabled the system to be built and the science department now uses it to teach about alternative energy sources. Another project is looking at the kinds of materials that may be used in the improvement of an area of the school grounds and the environmental implications of using different materials.

Work on energy resources and energy transfer in the **science** department links with the work on energy in other subjects. The department also uses the school grounds to link scientific theory with practice and has developed a role-play exercise on the effects of farming practices on local rivers and Sites of Special Scientific Interest, exploring conflicts of interest and possible alternatives.

The **mathematics** department has devised a course which uses spreadsheets showing statistics of energy use and population trends to explore some of the implications and consequences of these trends.

Alongside curriculum initiatives, the working party carried out an audit which focused attention on the litter problem at the school. It worked out the time and money spent on emptying bins and picking up litter. A scheme has been introduced to try to reduce this and to increase pupils' sense of control over their environment. Money saved (by lack of vandalism and damage to the school and by a reduction of time spent on dealing with litter) or raised (through recycling) is spent on needs identified by pupils through the school council.

EXAMPLE 28

| A secondary school of about 1200 pupils in northern England | Investigating different views on a controversial environmental issue |

A Year 10 **English** class used a computer package about an environmental issue, Brent Spar, to develop critical analysis, study ways of using language, develop understanding about decision making in environmental issues and use IT skills. The computer disk contains text, graphics and data illustrating the arguments presented by both Shell UK and Greenpeace about ways of disposing of the Brent Spar Oil Storage Buoy. Its purpose is to develop pupils' critical understanding of the social and economic context in which environmental controversies like Brent Spar occur.

The class spent three lessons and a homework focusing on the way in which language was used in the dispute between two large organisations. In small groups, half the class looked at Greenpeace materials, while the others studied the Shell press releases. The pupils, who had varying degrees of computer literacy, studied the text to identify words and phrases which would show the writers in a good light and others which would show the other side in a bad light. The language used was discussed and the class identified bias in the language and differing linguistic styles of the two protagonists. The groups then identified illustrations and cartoons to illustrate the side of the argument on which they were focusing.

After a review of findings, groups were asked to produce a display to illustrate the viewpoint they had been investigating. The activity provided opportunities for speaking and listening, reading and writing. It also provided clear links to work in **science** and **geography.**

KEY STAGE 4

The Brent Spar is laden with over 100 tonnes of toxic sludge and more than 30 tonnes of radioactive scale. It contains a lethal chemical cocktail including lead, arsenic, mercury, and PCB's which, if allowed to enter the marine environment, would present a considerable threat.

The dumping of the Brent Spar is wholly inconsistent with the best international practice in disposing of oil installations. In the Gulf of Mexico, where the dumping of redundant oil installations is prohibited by US Environmental Protection Laws, Shell practices far less environmentally damaging methods of disposal. Indeed, the fact that Shell would even consider such a form of disposal shows the utter contempt with which your UK arm is prepared to treat the environment – so long as it is able to get away with it.

Because of the protest which Greenpeace volunteers have mounted on the Brent Spar, Shell UK's plans have now become public knowledge. It is clear to all who read or hear about the issue that Shell UK has arrived at a decision to dump the Brent Spar based on what is best for the company's economic performance, not what is best for the environment.

- Shell UK is not predisposed to the offshore disposal of redundant installations simply to save costs. The Brent Spar storage and loading buoy is an unusual installation; and under UK Government policy – consistent with best international practice – the individual characteristics and circumstances of each disposal are carefully considered on a case-by-case basis. The responsible option in this case – on environmental, safety and health considerations – is carefully-managed deepwater disposal. But it is foreseen that future applications of the balanced case-by-case approach will lead to onshore recovery and scrapping for many subsequent disposals of redundant British installations.

Greenpeace advocate the option of onshore disposal and scrapping for the Brent Spar. This was rigorously evaluated in numerous engineering and environmental studies, many of them independent, carried out since the Spar was decommissioned in 1991. These studies have demonstrated that on balance there would be no environmental benefit while the safety and occupational health risks for the workforce involved in onshore disposal would be considerably greater.

- The same independent expert analysis confirms that the environmental impact of the deepwater disposal would be negligible, very localised, at more than 2000 metres (6000 ft) depth and some 240 kilometres (150 miles) from land, and inaccessible to the food chain. The alternative of controlled waste management on land would have at least the same environmental impact, albeit still negligible.

In this connection, I should add that references to "100 tonnes of toxic sludge", "a lethal chemical cocktail" and "considerable threat" are irresponsibly alarmist. At least 90% of the sludge is sand, and all but a tiny proportion of the rest is heavy stable oil residues — not dissimilar from the bitumen on our roads. The very low level of radioactivity from naturally occurring salts which have formed the scale on the inside of the Spar is no more than would emanate from a group of granite houses in Aberdeen. The proportion of heavy metals in the sludge is not significantly different from that which would occur naturally in the same weight of plankton or of marine sediments.

Conflicting views on the Brent Spar issue: extracts from correspondence between Greenpeace and Shell UK Ltd

EXAMPLE 29

A field studies centre in south west England, catering for pupils of all ages | Fieldwork with visually impaired pupils

Groups of visually impaired pupils from four schools visit the field centre each year for two-and-a-half days of **geography** GCSE fieldwork, including work on coasts, vegetation and soils, and settlement.

Those pupils who are totally blind bring their own braille machines and all essential documentary material is brailled in advance by the accompanying teachers. The pupils are organised into groups which have both blind and partially sighted members, and the fieldwork is designed so that some of the activities can be carried out by the totally blind pupils on their own, while others require the assistance of those with partial sight. Measurements and observations are recorded both on paper and into tape recorders. Teaching sites have been arranged so that access from a vehicle is reasonably easy, since some of the pupils also have physical disabilities.

KEY STAGE 4

In the field exercise on soils and vegetation, pupils study the changes in soil and vegetation in an upland valley. They are introduced to the idea that plants require different conditions and that vegetation will therefore change with changing soil type. One valley side is used to demonstrate changes in slope angle, vegetation and soil type. Each group of pupils measures the slope profile using a pantometer incorporating a braille protractor. Using a quadrat, they then record the percentage cover of a limited number of selected species by feeling the texture and shape of the vegetation. The plants which are successfully identified by touch are heather, bracken and soft rush. Soil profiles are investigated using augers, with the blind pupils judging texture while the partially sighted pupils record colour and measure pH using the standard soil testing kit.

Using the results, pupils are able to draw conclusions about the way in which vegetation changes from the top of the slope to the valley bottom, and how these changes are related to soil type.

Coasts: measuring pebbles

Vegetation and soils: using a quadrat to record the percentage cover of different species

EXAMPLE 30

| A secondary school of about 1400 pupils in a midlands town | Design & technology and the environment |

The **design & technology** department has, for a number of years, used materials, particularly green wood coppice, from sustainable sources and encouraged pupils to consider the environmental implications of both choice of materials and the use of appropriate technologies.

A number of GCSE design & technology projects have focused on designing aspects of the site of a new building at a local environmental education centre. The projects included designs for approach paths, vehicles for disabled visitors, bridges and a recycling centre. Not only were pupils designing for a real life situation but also for one where criteria of environmental impact and sympathetic use of materials for aesthetic reasons were important. Preliminary visits were made to the centre so that pupils could investigate the context of their design projects. This enabled them to gain knowledge of materials, products and systems designed with the environment in mind.

KEY STAGE 4

EXAMPLE 31

| A secondary school in a midlands city | Environmental monitoring in collaboration with a local industrial firm |

A long-term link with a local industrial firm has stimulated work on environmental monitoring, involving work in **science**, **geography** and (by virtue of a computerised monitoring link installed in the school) **information technology**.

Work on environmental monitoring involves studying the processes employed by the company and the environmental problems that result. Following a five-day teacher placement with the company, pupils visit the company regularly to see how the company monitors noise, dust, industrial effluent and gas, to meet Health and Safety Regulations. The environmental monitoring techniques applied in the industrial context are also applied within the school environment. The work provides opportunities for pupils to investigate environmental planning and management in geography, and materials and their properties in science.

The school and the company have also acquired an automatic weather station, which they use jointly. The station is located on the school roof and sends signals to a computer. The company needed a means of assessing weather conditions (to comply with requirements of the Environmental Pollution Act), while the school geography department uses the weather station for its GCSE work on weather and climate.

Teaching about the environment may occur in many different curriculum areas. Some curriculum Orders specify particular environmental matters to be taught, while others offer opportunities for work with an environmental emphasis. Work on the environment may also provide realistic and interesting contexts for developing skills required in a number of subjects.

The following tables set out the National Curriculum requirements and opportunities for work on environmental matters. The particular environmental matters to be taught are listed under a heading 'Required coverage', while examples of opportunities for environmental work are also identified. Teachers may find these tables helpful as a basis for discussion and a stimulus for devising work with an environmental focus.

ENGLISH

KEY STAGE 1

Opportunities

Throughout the three programmes of study, environmental issues provide stimulating and authentic contexts for oral and written work, for example:

Speaking and listening
- predicting outcomes and discussing possibilities (1a)
- asking and answering questions that clarify understanding and indicate thoughtfulness about the matter under discussion (2a)

Reading
- using reference materials for different purposes (2d)

Writing
- writing on subjects that are of interest and importance (1a)

KEY STAGE 2

Opportunities

Throughout the three programmes of study, environmental issues provide stimulating and authentic contexts for oral and written work, for example:

Speaking and listening
- participation in a wide range of drama activities (1d);
- listening carefully, recalling and representing important features of an argument, talk, presentation, reading, radio or television programme (2b)

Reading
- reading texts with challenging subject matter that broadens perspectives and extends thinking (1c)
- posing pertinent questions about topics being investigated (2c)

Writing
- writing for an extended range of readers (1b) using the characteristics of different kinds of writing (1c)

KEY STAGES 3 AND 4

Opportunities

Throughout the three programmes of study, environmental issues provide stimulating and authentic contexts for oral and written work, for example:

Speaking and listening
- talking for a range of purposes including consideration of ideas, literature and the media (1a)
- in discussion, taking different views into account, sifting, summarising and using relevant points, citing evidence and constructing persuasive arguments (2a)

Reading
- reading texts from other cultures and traditions that represent their distinctive voices and forms, and offer varied perspectives and subject matter (1c)
- responding imaginatively and intellectually to what they read (2b)

Writing
- writing for aesthetic and imaginative purposes, to inform others and to develop thinking (1b)
- taking notes from written and oral sources, summarising carefully and reporting accurately (2b)

MATHEMATICS

KEY STAGE 1

Opportunities

Various environments (classroom, playground, beyond school) could be contexts for mathematical learning and may be described effectively by mathematical techniques, for example:

- collecting, recording and interpreting data (Number/5b), for example a litter survey
- understanding and using patterns and properties of shape (Shape, Space and Measure (SSM)/2a-c)
- understanding and using properties of position and movement (SSM/3a,b)

KEY STAGE 2

Opportunities

Various environments (classroom, playground, beyond school) could be contexts for mathematical learning and may be described effectively by mathematical techniques, for example:

- applying measuring skills in a range of purposeful contexts (Shape, Space and Measure (SSM)/1e)
- understanding and using measures (SSM/4a-c)
- accessing and collecting data through undertaking purposeful enquiries (Handling Data/1b), for example surveys of journeys to school
- collecting, representing and interpreting data (Handling Data/2a-d), for example on a school's use of energy

KEY STAGES 3 AND 4

Opportunities

Various environments (classroom, playground, beyond school) could be contexts for mathematical learning and may be described effectively by mathematical techniques, for example:

- exploring shape and space through drawing and practical work (Shape, Space and Measure (SSM)/1b)
- developing an understanding of scale, including using and interpreting maps and drawings (SSM/3d), for example plans of the school grounds
- designing a questionnaire or an experiment to capture the data needed to follow lines of enquiry and to test hypotheses, taking into account possible bias (Handling Data/2b), for example a survey of energy use
- constructing appropriate diagrams and graphs (Handling Data/2c)

SCIENCE

KEY STAGE 1

Required coverage:
- relating understanding of science to domestic and environmental contexts (Introduction/2a)
- learning how to treat living things and the environment with care and sensitivity (Introduction/2c)
- learning that there are different kinds of plants and animals in the local environment (Life Processes and Living Things (LPLT)/5a)
- learning that there are differences between local environments and that these affect which animals and plants are found there (LPLT/5b)

Opportunities include:
- experimenting and investigating in environmental contexts (Experimental and Investigative Science/1–3)
- studying life processes (LPLT/1)
- studying green plants as organisms (LPLT/3)
- making and detecting sounds (Physical Processes/3c-e)

KEY STAGE 2

Required coverage:
- considering ways in which living things and the environment need protection (Introduction/2d)
- learning that different plants and animals are found in different habitats (Life Processes and Living Things (LPLT)/5a)
- learning how animals and plants in two different habitats are suited to their environment (LPLT/5b)
- learning that food chains show feeding relationships in an ecosystem (LPLT/5c)
- learning that nearly all food chains start with a green plant (LPLT/5d)
- learning that micro-organisms exist and that many may be beneficial while others may be harmful (LPLT/5e)

Opportunities include:
- experimenting and investigating in environmental contexts (Experimental and Investigative Science/1–3)
- learning that plant growth is affected by the availability of light and water, and by temperature (LPLT/3a)

KEY STAGE 3

Required coverage:

- relating scientific knowledge and understanding to the care of living things and of the environment (Introduction/2c)
- considering the benefits and drawbacks of scientific and technological developments in environmental and other contexts (Introduction/2d)
- learning that variation within a species can have both environmental and inherited causes (Life Processes and Living Things (LPLT)/4b)
- learning that different habitats support different plants and animals (LPLT/5a)
- learning how some organisms are adapted to survive daily and seasonal changes in their habitats (LPLT/5b)
- learning that in food webs there are several food chains with species in common (LPLT/5d)
- learning how toxic materials may accumulate in food chains (LPLT/5e)
- learning about factors affecting the size of populations (LPLT/5f)
- learning that organisms successfully competing in their environment contribute relatively more offspring to the next generation (LPLT/5g)
- learning how rocks are weathered (Materials and their Properties (MP)/2f)
- learning about the rock cycle (MP/2g)
- learning about the classification of rocks, their texture and mineral composition (MP/2h)
- learning about the possible effects that burning fossil fuels has on the environment (MP/2p)
- learning how acids in the atmosphere can lead to corrosion of metal and chemical weathering of rock (MP/3i)
- learning about energy resources (Physical Processes/5a–d)

Opportunities include:

- experimenting and investigating in environmental contexts (Experimental and Investigative Science (EIS)/1–4), especially the consideration of contexts, for example fieldwork, where variables cannot readily be controlled (EIS/1g)
- learning about nutrition and growth of green plants (LPLT/3a–e)
- learning about chemical reactions that are generally not useful (MP/2n)

KEY STAGE 4

(The requirements and opportunities shown below refer to both Single and Double Science, unless they are shown in bold type, in which case references are to Double Science only)

Required coverage:

- considering ways in which science is applied and used, and evaluating the benefits and drawbacks of scientific and technological developments for individuals, communities and environments (Introduction/2a)
- using scientific knowledge and understanding to evaluate the effects of some applications of science on health and on the quality of life (Introduction/2b)
- relating scientific knowledge and understanding to the care of living things and of the environment (Introduction/2c)
- considering competing priorities and the decisions that have to be made about energy requirements, taking into account social, economic and environmental factors (Introduction/2d)

- considering the power and limitations of science in addressing industrial, social and environmental issues and some of the ethical dilemmas involved (Introduction/2e)
- studying living things in their environment (Life Processes and Living Things (LPLT)/4 – Single; LPLT/5 – Double), in particular learning:
  - how the impact of human activity on the environment is related to population size, economic factors and industrial requirements (LPLT/4b – Single; LPLT/5b – Double)
  - **learning how energy is transferred through an ecosystem (LPLT/5d)**
  - **learning about the role of microbes in the decomposition of organic materials (LPLT/5e)**
- **studying changing materials (Materials and their Properties (MP)/2), in particular learning:**
  - **how nitrogenous fertilisers affect the environment (MP/2q)**
  - **how the carbon cycle helps maintain atmospheric composition (MP/2w)**
- learning the meaning of energy efficiency and about the need for economical use of energy resources (Physical Processes (PP)/5e)
- learning that there is background radioactivity (PP/6b)

Opportunities include:
- using environmental contexts for experimental and investigative work (Experimental and Investigative Science (EIS/1–4))
- recognising contexts, for example fieldwork, where variables cannot readily be controlled (EIS/1g)
- **studying green plants as organisms (LPLT/3), in particular learning:**
  - **about factors affecting rates of photosynthesis (LPLT/3b)**
  - **about the hormonal control of plant growth (LPLT/3c)**
- studying living things in their environment (LPLT/4 – Single; LPLT/5 – Double), in particular learning:
  - how the distribution and relative abundance of organisms in a habitat can be explained in terms of adaptation, competition and predation (LPLT/4a – Single; LPLT/5a – Double)
  - **how to describe the food chain using pyramids of numbers and pyramids of biomass (LPLT/5c)**
- studying changing materials (MP/1 – Single; MP/2 – Double), in particular learning:
  - about the use as fuels of some of the products from crude oil distillation (MP/1c – Single; MP/2c – Double)
  - about the products of burning hydrocarbons (MP/1d – Single; MP/2d – Double)
  - **about geological influences on the environment (MP/2x,z)**
- learning about energy resources and transfer (PP/5b,c,d)
- studying radioactivity (PP/6), in particular learning about:
  - the beneficial and harmful effects of radiation on matter and living organisms (PP/6f)

DESIGN & TECHNOLOGY

KEY STAGE 1

Opportunities include:

- working with a range of materials and components, for example reclaimed materials (2a)
- relating the way things work to their intended purpose, how materials and components have been used, people's needs and what users say about them (5d)
- considering the hazards and risks in activities (5f)

KEY STAGE 2

Opportunities include:

- working with a (wider) range of materials (2a)
- relating the way things work to their intended purpose, how materials and components have been used, people's needs and what users say about them (5g)
- considering the effectiveness of a product, including the extent to which it uses resources appropriately (5i)

KEY STAGE 3

Required coverage:

- judging a technological product in terms of its impact beyond the purpose for which it was designed, for example on the environment (9d)

Opportunities include:

- considering the needs and values of intended users (3d)
- considering the aesthetics, function, safety, reliability and cost of designs (3f)
- taking responsibility for recognising hazards in a range of products, activities and environments with which pupils are familiar (10a)

KEY STAGE 4

Required coverage:

- recognising that moral, economic, social, cultural and environmental issues can make conflicting demands when designing (3d)
- judging the quality of a product in terms of:
  - whether it is an appropriate use of resources (8c)
  - its impact beyond the purpose for which it was designed, for example on the environment (8d)

Opportunities include:

- taking responsibility for recognising hazards in products, activities and environments, including the unfamiliar (9a)
- managing the environment and justifying the action taken to control the risk (9c)

INFORMATION TECHNOLOGY

KEY STAGE 1

Opportunities include:

- exploring the use of computer systems and control technology in everyday life (1b)
- communicating and handling information (2c)
- looking at the use of IT in the outside world (1c), considering whether the technology is 'environmentally friendly'
- using IT-based models or simulations to explore aspects of real and imaginary situations (3c)

KEY STAGE 2

Opportunities include:

- investigating parallels with the use of IT in the wider world, considering the effects of such uses and comparing them with other methods (1d)
- communicating and handling information (especially 2b–d)
- controlling and monitoring an aspect of the environment (3a,b)
- using the environment as a context for simulations (3c,d)

KEY STAGE 3

Opportunities include:

- discussing some of the social, economic, ethical and moral issues raised by IT (1f)
- communicating and handling information (2c-e)
- controlling and measuring (3c), for example an aspect of the environment
- modelling, using the environment as a context (3d–f)

KEY STAGE 4

Opportunities include:

- recognising the impact of new technologies on methods of working in the outside world, and on social, economic, ethical and moral issues (1e, 2c)
- communicating and handling information (2d)
- controlling, measuring and modelling (3a,b), for example using the environment as the subject or as a context

HISTORY

At all key stages the Key Elements offer opportunities to study environmental issues.

1. Chronology, for example placing changes to the made environment in a chronological framework
2. Range and depth of historical understanding, for example analysing features of periods, including the made environment; describing and explaining situations and changes; making links between periods
3. Interpretations of history, for example looking at how changes to the made environment have been analysed differently
4. Historical enquiry, for example investigating the past, including sites and buildings
5. Organisation and communication, for example communicating information and using terminology such as 'industrialisation'

KEY STAGE 1

Opportunities include:
- the everyday life, work and leisure and culture of men, women and children in the past (1a,b), for example types of fuel used in heating, methods of washing

KEY STAGE 2

Opportunities include:
- studying the impact of settlement (Romans, Anglo Saxons and Vikings in Britain – Study Unit 1/a–c)
- studying life in town and country (Life in Tudor times – Study Unit 2/e,f)
- considering the impact of industrialisation (Victorian Britain – Study Unit 3a/a–d; Britain since 1930 – Study Unit 3b/a–d)
- studying the impact of modern technology and transport, including the car (Britain since 1930 – Study Unit 3b/a–d)
- studying environmental change in the locality (Local history – Study Unit 5)

KEY STAGE 3

Opportunities include:
- learning about changes in town and countryside (The making of the United Kingdom 1500–1750 – Study Unit 2/c)
- considering the impact of the neolithic revolution (An era or turning point in European history before 1914 – Study Unit 5/b,c)
- studying attitudes of people to the environment and how they shaped and were shaped by their environment (A past non-European society – Study Unit 6/a,b)

KEY STAGE 4

There is no programme of study for Key Stage 4, but GCSE Criteria require all syllabuses to focus on:
- key issues, events, personalities and developments in the periods and topics specified (4.2 i)
- the key features and characteristics of the periods, societies or situations specified and, where appropriate, the social, cultural, religious and ethnic diversity of the societies studied (4.2 ii)
- history from a variety of perspectives, including economic, social and cultural, technological, scientific, religious and aesthetic (4.2 v)
- history through a range of sources of information, including buildings and sites (4.2 vi)

GEOGRAPHY

KEY STAGE 1

Required coverage:

- undertaking fieldwork activities in the locality of the school (3b)
- studying the main physical and human features of two localities (5a)
- studying how land and buildings are used in two localities (5d)
- expressing views on the attractive and unattractive features of the environment in a locality (6a), investigating how that environment is changing (6b) and how its quality can be sustained and improved (6c)

Opportunities include:

- investigating the effects of weather on people and their surroundings (5c)

KEY STAGE 2

Required coverage:

- studying the main physical and human features and environmental issues that give three localities their character (5a)
- investigating how features of these localities influence the nature and location of human activities within them (5c)
- learning how people affect the environment (10a) and how and why people seek to manage and sustain their environment (10b)

Opportunities include:

- learning how land in settlements is used in different ways (9b)
- investigating a particular issue arising from the way land is used (9c)
- studying weather conditions in different parts of the world (8c)

KEY STAGE 3

Required coverage:

- considering the issues that arise from people's interaction with their environments (1c)
- studying the physical and human features that give rise to the distinctive characteristics and regional variety of two countries (5a)
- studying the characteristics of two regions in each of the countries (5b)
- learning about the characteristics of one type of vegetation (10a) and how that type of vegetation is related to climate, soil and human activity (10b)
- investigating why some areas are viewed as being of great scenic attraction and how conflicting demands on the areas can arise (15a)
- learning how attempts are made to plan and manage such environments (15b)
- learning how considerations of sustainable development, stewardship and conservation affect environmental planning and management (15c)
- studying either water supply or energy supply and its environmental implications (15d or e)

Opportunities include:

- learning how population and resources are interrelated (11c)
- investigating how conflicts can arise over the use of land (12d)
- studying the effects of changes in the distribution of economic activity (13b)
- learning about differences in development and their effect on quality of life (14b)

KEY STAGE 4

There is no programme of study at Key Stage 4, but GCSE Criteria state that all syllabuses must require:

- development of a sense of place and an appreciation of the environment (2.1 ii)
- study of the interrelationships between people and the environment (4.1 v)
- study of the geographical aspects of social, economic, political and environmental issues (4.1 vi)
- study of the significance and effects of attitudes and values in the management of environments (4.1 vii)

MODERN FOREIGN LANGUAGES

KEY STAGES 3 AND 4 (NO PoS FOR KEY STAGES 1 AND 2)

Required coverage:

- studying the world around us (Part IIC), notably the natural and made environment
- studying the international world (Part IIE), notably life in other countries and communities

Opportunities include:

- considering pupils' own culture and comparing it with the cultures of the countries and communities where the target language is spoken (Part I/4c)
- identifying with the experiences and perspectives of people in these countries and communities (Part IIC)
- studying the home town and local area, and people, places and customs (Part IIC)
- studying world events and issues (Part IIE)

ART

KEY STAGE 1

Required coverage:

- recording responses, including observations of the natural and made environment (7a, 8a)
- identifying in the school and the locality the work of artists, craftspeople and designers (9a)

Opportunities include:

- experimenting with visual elements to make images and artefacts (8e)

KEY STAGE 2

Required coverage:

- developing skills for recording from direct experience and imagination and selecting and recording from first-hand observation (7a, 8a)
- identifying in the school and the locality the materials and methods used by artists, craftspeople and designers (9a)

Opportunities include:

- recording observations and ideas, and collecting visual evidence and information, using a sketchbook (8b)

KEY STAGE 3

Required coverage:
- recording responses, including observations of the natural and made environment (7a, 8a)
- relating art, craft and design to its social, historical and cultural context (9c)

Opportunities include:
- selecting and recording observations and ideas, researching and organising a range of visual evidence and information, using a sketchbook (8b)

KEY STAGE 4

There is no programme of study at Key Stage 4, but GCSE Criteria require all syllabuses to include:
- recording from direct experience, observation and imagination (3.1 i)
- identifying the distinctive characteristics of art, craft and design and relating them to the context in which the work was created (3.1 v)

MUSIC

KEY STAGE 1

Opportunities include:
- developing awareness of venue (4b)
- composing in response to a variety of stimuli (4c), for example sounds from the environment
- using sounds to create musical effects (5g)

KEY STAGE 2

Opportunities include:
- developing awareness of venue (4b)
- composing in response to a variety of stimuli (4c), for example sounds from the environment
- using sounds and structures to achieve an intended effect (5g), for example to create a particular atmosphere

KEY STAGE 3

Opportunities include:
- developing a sense of venue (4b)
- composing in response to a variety of stimuli (4c), for example sounds from the environment
- identify ways in which personal response is influenced by the environment in which the music takes place (6b)

KEY STAGE 4

There is no programme of study at Key Stage 4, but GCSE Criteria require all syllabuses to include:
- opportunities for pupils to promote their cultural development and involvement in music as performers, composers and listeners through the study of a wide range of music which reflects the richness of our cultural heritage (2.1 ii)

PHYSICAL EDUCATION

KEY STAGE 1

Required coverage:

- using indoor and outdoor environments where appropriate to the teaching of the area of activity (PoS rubric)

Opportunities include:

- performing movements or patterns, including some from existing dance traditions (3b), considering the environments in which the traditions developed

KEY STAGE 2

Required coverage:

- performing outdoor and adventurous activities, for example orienteering exercises, in one or more different environments (5a), for example school grounds, woodland, and developing the skills necessary for the activities undertaken (5c)

Opportunities include:

- undertaking challenges of a physical and problem-solving nature (5b)

KEY STAGE 3

Required coverage:

- performing at least one outdoor and adventurous activity (5), either on or off the school site (5a,d)

KEY STAGE 4

Required coverage:

- undertaking outdoor and adventurous activities (5):
  - preparing for and undertaking a journey in an unfamiliar environment (5a)
  - learning about the effects of nutrition and climatic conditions on the body and becoming aware of and responding to changing environmental conditions (5d)

RELIGIOUS EDUCATION

Agreed Syllabuses for religious education are defined locally. Model syllabuses published by SCAA 'suggest' rather than 'direct' content and structure for teaching religious education; the opportunities set out below are those offered by the model syllabuses.

KEY STAGE 1

Opportunities

- content, for example:
  - listening to stories and poems which describe God as the creator and the idea of the world as a precious gift to humanity
- learning experiences, for example:
  - talking about their own feelings about the natural world, such as awe, wonder and a sense of mystery
  - distinguishing between what is made and what belongs to the natural world

KEY STAGE 2

Opportunities

● content, for example:
  – learning about Islamic teaching that humans are the best of Allah's creation
  – learning about Sikh teaching that God is One, the Creator and Sustainer and that all human beings are equal in the eyes of God
● learning experiences, for example:
  – considering Christian (and other) beliefs about God as creator
  – talking about their attitudes towards the environment
  – considering how they can show their respect for the environment

KEY STAGE 3

Opportunities

● content, for example:
  – learning how Christian values are demonstrated through social and global issues
  – learning about Buddhist teachings about the causes of suffering in the world and how it might be overcome
  – learning about Hindu beliefs about the cyclical nature of time and space
● learning experiences, for example:
  – talking about Christian responses to the cycle of development in the natural world and in human life
  – exploring ways in which the natural world has inspired spirituality

KEY STAGE 4

Opportunities

● content, for example:
  – learning about the Assisi Declarations and what they have to say about religious attitudes towards the environment
  – learning about Jewish teaching on *tikkun olam* (mending the world) and how this affects contemporary Jewish attitudes towards green issues
● learning experiences, for example:
  – reflecting on the teachings of religions on environmental issues
  – considering how care for the environment may be supported philosophically without applying to religion for authority

GCSE Religious Studies
Subject criteria make no explicit references to environmental matters, but offer opportunities for their study. For example, a course should:

● identify and promote exploration of, and reflection upon, questions about the meaning and purpose of life (2.2 ii)
● consider religious and, where appropriate, other responses to moral issues (2.2 iv)

ACKNOWLEDGEMENTS

SCAA wishes to thank all those who contributed to the preparation of this guidance for schools. Special thanks are due to the advisory group, which included representatives from schools, LEAs, the Council for Environmental Education, the Royal Society for the Protection of Birds, the National Association for Environmental Education, and OFSTED. Thanks are also due to the primary schools, secondary schools and others, including World Wide Fund for Nature, the Field Studies Council and Learning Through Landscapes, who contributed case-study materials, photographs and ideas.

SCAA is particularly grateful to those schools which have agreed that their examples can be included in this document:

Bamford County Primary School, Derbyshire; Boundstone Community College, Lancing; Broadway East First School, Newcastle; Camm's Endowed C of E (Aided) Primary School, Eckington; Canterbury Environmental Education Centre; Cowick First School, Exeter; Droitwich High School; FSC at Flatford Mill, East Bergholt; Forest Gate Community School, Newham; Gosforth Park First School, Newcastle; Gosforth East Middle School, Newcastle; Grangewood School, Hillingdon; Greenshaw High School, Sutton; Hawtonville Junior School, Newark; Hilton County Primary School, Derby; Holmfirth Junior Infant and Nursery School, Huddersfield; Kingsmead School, Hackney; Langtoft County Primary School, Lincolnshire; Mulberry School for Girls, Tower Hamlets; FSC at Nettlecombe Court, Williton; Newquay Tretherras School; Our Lady and St Anne's RC Primary School, Newcastle; Panshanger Junior and Mixed Infant School, Welwyn Garden City; Raincliffe School, Scarborough; Royton and Crompton School, Oldham; St Oswald's RC Primary School, Newcastle; St Peter's CE School, Hammersmith; Samuel Ward Upper School, Haverhill; Sandon High School, Stoke-on-Trent; Saxon Hill School, Lichfield; Selwood Anglican/Methodist Middle School, Frome; Sinfin Community School, Derby; Stanley Grove Infant School, Manchester; Tadcaster Grammar School; Taxal & Fernilee CE Primary School, Derbyshire; Theale Green School, Reading; Ysgol Gynradd Tregarth, Gwynedd.